Biography

Tiger **WOODS**

Jeremy Roberts

Lerner Publications Company
Minneapolis

Copyright © 2002 by Jim DeFelice

This book is available in two editions:
Library binding by Lerner Publications Company,
  a division of Lerner Publishing Group
Soft cover by First Avenue Editions,
  an imprint of Lerner Publishing Group
241 First Avenue North
Minneapolis, MN 55401 U.S.A.

Website address: www.lernerbooks.com

Library of Congress Cataloging-in-Publication Data

Roberts, Jeremy
    Tiger Woods / by Jeremy Roberts.
      p.   cm. — (A & E biography)
    Includes index.
    Summary: Examines the life and performance of golfer Tiger Woods.
    ISBN: 0–8225–0030–2 (lib. bdg. : alk. paper)
    ISBN: 0–8225–0386–7 (pbk. : alk. paper)
  1. Woods, Tiger—Juvenile literature. 2. Golfers—United
States—Biography—Juvenile literature. [1. Woods, Tiger.
2. Golfers. 3. Racially mixed people—Biography.] I. Title.
II. Biography (Lerner Publications Company)
GV964.W66 R63 2002
796.352'092—dc21   2001003830

Manufactured in the United States of America
1 2 3 4 5 6 – JR – 07 06 05 04 03 02

CONTENTS

At only eleven months old, Tiger already looked comfortable on the putting green. Although he's holding the club with his left hand, the boy turned out to be a right-handed player.

PROLOGUE

The little boy slipped down from the highchair, toddling toward his father in the garage of their California home. His dad looked over in amazement as the nine-month-old picked up the golf club he had received as a toy. Father and son had spent many sessions out in the garage these past three months. Dad would launch practice shots into a net as the baby watched.

Usually, the little boy just cooed and smiled. But on this day, the baby picked up the small golf club his father had cut down for him. Then, on unsteady feet, the toddler approached one of the balls on the practice carpet. He pulled his golf club back, waved it slightly as his daddy had, and swung like an expert. The ball flew into the net.

"We have a genius on our hands!" the excited father told his wife after that swing.

Perhaps it was a lucky shot. Perhaps it was fate. Perhaps over time that first swing has come to seem better than it really was. But no matter—the toddler's early tee shot was an omen. The child was Tiger Woods. Over the next twenty years, he would develop into the finest golfer the world has ever known.

Of course, at the time no one knew how great Tiger Woods would be. The odds against any athlete are immense. Even someone with great natural talent can be

In 1990 Tiger posed with his parents, Earl and Kultida, who have long been a source of stability and support for the talented young athlete.

distracted or suffer misfortune. He or she will certainly be discouraged along the way. Often it is difficult to tell exactly what helps and what hurts a young
person's development.

Tiger Woods faced one obstacle many golfers never
encounter. Tiger's dad is African American. His
mother comes from Thailand. While American society has changed greatly since the civil rights battles
of the 1950s and 1960s, prejudice remains. This is
true in sports, despite the efforts and achievements
of many.

By the time Tiger picked up his golf club, black stars were common in baseball, basketball, and football. However, golf had never had a black superstar. Relatively few blacks played professional golf. In fact, in many places, blacks were still openly discouraged from playing the game, even for recreation.

But prejudice would not hold back Tiger Woods. With talent, hard work, and a great deal of love and support from his parents, he overcame the odds to become one of the greatest athletes of all time. And he's getting better.

Charlie Sifford was the first African American golfer on the Professional Golfers' Association (PGA) Tour, joining it in 1960. He enjoyed even more success on the Senior Tour.

An American Green Beret, right, and a South Vietnamese
soldier help a wounded soldier reach a helicopter. Earl Woods,
Tiger's dad, was an officer in the Green Berets, the top-notch
special forces unit of the U.S. Army. During the Vietnam War,
he served two tours of duty in the late 1960s and early 1970s.

Chapter **ONE**

BIRTH OF A LEGEND

MAJOR EARL WOODS LEANED BACK IN THE BAM-boo thicket. A sniper had just missed killing him. Woods decided he needed a few minutes of quiet. But this was Vietnam. The country had been at war for nearly three decades. No place was ever really safe, especially in the early 1970s.

"Woody!" yelled a voice. "Don't move!"

Woods didn't.

"There's a bamboo viper about two inches from your right eye," said the man, South Vietnamese army colonel Vuong Dang Phong, who had warned him.

Phong coaxed his friend to keep still for several more minutes as one of the most dangerous snakes in the world slid a few inches from his face. One wrong move—even a hiccup or a sneeze—and the snake could have seriously injured or killed Woods and Phong. Finally, the snake slipped away. Woods beat a quick retreat.

It was neither the first nor last time that the two men faced danger together. Major Woods was an excellent soldier and would earn a special medal for his bravery, but it was Phong he considered special. He began calling the Vietnamese colonel Tiger. The nickname was a tribute to Phong's bravery.

Earl Woods was in Vietnam in 1970 for his second assignment in the war-torn country. By then, U.S. troops had been in South Vietnam for more than ten years, trying to help the government in its fight against the Communist North Vietnamese. Woods was a Green Beret major. His job was to help the South Vietnamese improve their army so they could defend themselves better. The war was not very popular in the United States, but soldiers like Earl Woods believed that their fight would help keep Communism from spreading.

Woods soon went home. America eventually withdrew all of its troops. South Vietnam was defeated by North Vietnam. But Earl Woods would never forget the man who saved his life.

ELDRICK "TIGER" WOODS

By 1974 Earl Woods, who had been promoted to lieutenant colonel, was ready to retire from the army and rejoin civilian life. He had married a woman from Thailand named Kultida Punswad in 1973 and wanted to settle down with her in the United States. Kultida—often called Tida by family and friends—had met Earl when he was stationed in Bangkok a few years earlier. They had fallen in love almost immediately.

Kultida is Earl's second wife. Though Earl and his first wife had two sons and a daughter, they divorced.

Earl met Kultida in Bangkok, the large, bustling capital of Thailand.

Kultida Woods's philosophy of life is based on Buddhism, the main religion practiced in Thailand. Through his mom, Tiger came to understand the importance of having respect for others and of sharing one's good fortune.

A few months before Earl left the army, another officer introduced him to golf. In a few months, Earl became a fanatic. Very competitive by nature, he spent hours and hours practicing, determined to beat his friend. Finally he challenged him to a match—and won. Earl continued to hone his game after taking a job as a contracts administrator with McDonnell Douglas, a large company in California.

He was still improving when his new son was born on December 30, 1975. The boy was named Eldrick, a unique name that begins with his father's first initial and ends with his mother's. Kultida said that she gave him that name so that he would be surrounded by both parents throughout his life. Right from the start, Earl called the infant Tiger, in honor of the man who had saved his life in Vietnam.

A Natural

Both Kultida and Earl doted on their son. According to Earl, Kultida's Asian background played an important role in shaping Tiger. "The way Tiger was taught to respect his parents and other adults, to rely on his instincts and feelings, to be unselfish and generous," said Earl, "these are all tenets of Asian philosophy and culture that he has embraced."

Tiger also embraced golf, which he began "studying" in the garage at about six months old. His father had no intention of teaching the infant the game so early; he just brought him along while he practiced.

Small children rarely have much upper-body strength or coordination. Both are important in golf, especially when driving, or hitting the ball far down the fairway (the part of a golf course between the tee and the green). According to his father, Tiger displayed that

natural ability from a very young age. He also quickly
learned how to use different types of swings to send
the ball high or far. Even before he could read, said
his dad, Tiger could recognize swings well enough to
say that someone had a reverse pivot, or a flaw in his
swing.

Instead of carrying a rattle, said Earl, Tiger "had a
putter." Soon after Tiger learned how to walk, he accompanied his dad to the Navy Golf Course in Los
Alamitas, near their home in Cypress, California. Earl
had special clubs made for Tiger and began showing
him how to play. When he was about two, Tiger even
memorized his father's office phone number and
would call to ask if they could play golf after work.
Father and son were soon regulars on the course.

In golf, competitors measure themselves against a
score, called par, and try to get a lower score. Earl

HOLE		1	2	3	4	5	6	7	
BLUE	M: 70.0/122 L: 75.8/131	379	390	148	513	202	422	504	
WHITE	M: 68.8/119 L: 74.5/128	365	380	129	500	191	407	480	
HANDICAP		11	3	17	5	13	1	7	
	We				·				
PAR		4	4	3	5	3	4	5	

Golf shots are recorded on a scorecard. When Tiger was
young, Earl invented a scoring system just for him.

soon established a special scoring system to make the game more interesting for Tiger. This "Tiger par" system showed the young golfer how many shots it should take him to sink the ball in a hole.

Tiger's talents went beyond athleticism. He began memorizing multiplication tables when he was three years old. He soon mastered basic math. He seemed happy and willing to please adults who took an interest in him, and he would often demonstrate his golf prowess.

He also learned to deal with attention. He had to, because word soon spread that pint-sized Tiger Woods was a golf prodigy.

At eighteen months, Tiger was already showing his boyish grin. Within a few months, he was wowing audiences on television with his extraordinary skill.

Chapter **TWO**

EARLY DAYS

TIGER WOODS WALKED QUICKLY FROM THE SIDE OF the stage toward the lights. Not yet three, he didn't completely understand what was going on, but he did know one thing—he was there to hit a golf ball.

Television talk show host Mike Douglas waved him forward with a friendly grin. Douglas introduced Tiger and his dad to the audience and then helped little Tiger find the right spot on the fake golf course green at center stage. He stood back as Tiger waved his specially sized golf club.

The ball sailed long and straight—a perfect drive.

Tiger wasn't done. Douglas called out one of his guests, the famous comedian Bob Hope. Hope's comedy routines and appearances often included jokes about golf. Hope aped for the camera, asking the little boy, with a wink, if he had any money to place a bet. But it was Tiger who stole the show. Challenged to a putting competition, he agreed—then grabbed his ball and plopped it down half an inch from the hole. The audience cracked up.

PREJUDICE

Tiger's trip to *The Mike Douglas Show* in 1977 was one of several television appearances during his days as a preschooler and young boy. He went on such shows as *That's Incredible*. Viewers were surprised that such a young child could swing golf clubs so perfectly, especially under the glare of TV lights. People would laugh or think he was very cute. A few were impressed by his powerful and well-balanced swing. But most viewers probably thought he was just an interesting and unusual child who would eventually tire of golf and show biz.

Off camera, however, Tiger's golf skills were growing. When Tiger was four, the Navy Golf Course limited his play. The officials said it was because of his age, but Earl believed it was because he and his son were black.

Like many American sports and institutions, golf has a history of prejudice against minorities. Private clubs own many golf courses. To play at a course regularly, a person has to be a member of the club. In most cases, membership is very expensive, which keeps some minorities from joining.

DRIVING PAST PREJUDICE

Until the early 1970s, PGA rules made it difficult for minority golfers to qualify to compete in major events. A black man did not compete at the Masters Tournament until Lee Elder made the field in 1975. But, as Tiger often points out, he was not the first African American golfer to do well. Among earlier PGA achievers are:

Jim Dent was not considered a standout as a member of the PGA Tour. But as a member of the Senior Tour, a series of separate events for older golfers, Dent has been a star. Since 1989, he has taken away more than $5 million in prize money and has notched more than ten titles.

Robert Lee Elder, generally known as Lee Elder, ranks as one of the finest golfers ever. Best known as the first black to play at the Masters, Elder notched more than $1 million in winnings on the PGA Tour. Among his most memorable matches was a dramatic sudden-death playoff against Jack Nicklaus at the American Golf Classic in 1968, Elder's first year on the tour. Nicklaus edged him out on the fifth hole in one of the tightest showdowns Nicklaus ever faced.

Calvin Peete turned pro in the 1970s and joined the PGA Tour full-time when he was in his early 30s. Despite different ailments, including an elbow he broke as a youth, Peete managed a dozen tournament victories and twice made the prestigious Ryder Cup team, which competes internationally for the United States. His winnings on the PGA Tour topped $2.3 million.

Charlie Sifford joined the PGA Tour in 1960. Among his victories were the Greater Hartford Open in 1967 and the Los Angeles Open in 1969. His career earnings on the PGA Tour were $341,344. He had considerable success on the PGA Senior Tour. Sifford detailed his life and struggles to overcome prejudice in the book *Just Let Me Play*.

Some clubs also have strict rules about who will be accepted for membership. In some cases, the rules or informal practices kept blacks and other minorities from joining. Even when they were allowed to play, they were often discriminated against with late starting times, which sometimes meant they played their final holes in the dark. While these practices changed during the 1960s, there was still much discrimination against blacks at golf courses and clubs during the late 1970s.

At the navy course, all retired military officers were allowed to play, including Earl. But rules prohibited children under ten from playing. At first, the rules did not seem to be enforced for anyone. Then suddenly, club officials cited the rules to keep Tiger out.

Earl Woods, whose ancestors included Native Americans and European Americans as well as blacks, had experienced prejudice for many years, on and off the golf course. He had encountered biased officers in the army. When the family first moved into the California neighborhood where Tiger was raised, for example, someone shot at their house with a BB gun. Sometimes members at the military golf club called Earl "Sergeant Brown," a not-so-subtle reference to the color of his skin.

"It was inconceivable to them that a black guy could rise above the rank of sergeant," said Earl. As a lieutenant colonel, he outranked many, if not all, of his detractors. He had served in an elite unit and put his life on the line in Vietnam not once but twice—

extreme measures of heroism by anyone's standards. But Earl said that this didn't stop some members from disliking him and his family and trying to hurt them.

TIGER'S ATTITUDE ABOUT RACE

Earl had learned to deal with prejudice throughout his life, first as a college baseball player and then as an army officer. His philosophy could be summed up in one word: perseverance. Kultida had similar beliefs. Both passed this attitude on to Tiger.

Tiger and his dad have long enjoyed a close relationship. Through Earl, Tiger learned to persevere no matter what obstacles might be in the way.

When it came to race and culture, Tiger thought of himself as a combination of many different backgrounds. He valued his father's African, European, and Native American background. He also felt close to his mother's Asian heritage. Growing up, he came to think of himself as a conglomeration of all these cultures. Tiger came up with a word to describe the mixture by combining the words *Caucasian, Black, Indian,* and *Asian.* The word was "cablinasian."

"The bottom line is that I am an American," he would tell reporters years later. "And proud of it."

MOZART

Rules or racial prejudice weren't about to stop the Woodses. Tiger's mother decided to find another course where he could play. She found Heartwell Golf Park, a small course in Long Beach, California, roughly fifteen miles from their home. One of the professionals at the course, whose job it was to help golfers, asked to see Tiger play.

"I was blown away," said the golf pro, Rudy Duran. "It was unbelievable. He was awesome. He had a perfect address position and took his club back into a perfect position at the top of the swing and smacked the ball, time after time. I felt he was like Mozart."

Duran's comparison was incredibly accurate. Wolfgang Amadeus Mozart is best known for his beautiful operas and other compositions that he wrote as an adult. But as a child, he performed on the harpsichord and other instruments for the royalty of Europe in the mid-eighteenth century. All serious music lovers of his time knew who he was.

Amazed that a four-year-old could control his club well enough to hit a ball high, low, or medium, Duran began teaching Tiger. Like Earl, he set Tiger pars for each hole based on Tiger's ability. Even though Woods was only four, Tiger par for the entire course was only 13 shots higher than an adult's. By the time he was five, Tiger had beaten his par by eight shots. He had also graduated to a full set of clubs, specially sized for his small body. He continued to hone his game, playing with Duran, Earl, and anyone else who cared to be amazed.

"The best thing about those practices was that my father always kept it fun," Tiger recalled later. "Golf for me has always been a labor of love and pleasure."

In some ways, said Tiger's father, the discrimination at the navy course helped Tiger, because it led him to Heartwell, where he could work on his game. His years there provided basic training that would pay off big in the future.

"Strange how unwelcome, unforeseen circumstances can shape our lives," Earl said.

COMPETITIONS

Baseball has T-ball and then Little League. Football has Pop Warner. In the golf world, junior competitions and tournaments are held across the country.

The American Junior Golf Association sponsors a series of national events for golfers in similar age groups. The competition can be fierce.

Tiger joined the Southern California Junior Golf Association when he was just four years old. The lowest age bracket was ten and under, so at first he played against much older kids. His first win came in his fourth match, against a ten-year-old.

At four, Tiger became a member of the Southern California Junior Golf Association and often competed against kids much older than he was.

Already, Tiger and his family were taking the sport very seriously. They made sacrifices for him to play and compete. The tournaments cost money to enter. They were sometimes held far away and at very early hours.

"He never complained when the alarm went off," said Earl years later. "I can still remember cracking one eye at 4 A.M. . . . [Kultida] and Tiger were preparing to leave for a nine-hole tournament a 90-minute drive away."

Tiger did very well during the weekend and summer matches, though he did not always win. By the time he was in second grade, he had already played and won an international tournament, or tourney, against kids from all over the world. His skills grew as he practiced and competed.

As he grew, his aptitude for the sport became more and more obvious. Earl Woods promised Tiger he would have "as good a chance as any of those country club kids" to succeed at the sport. But lessons and tournaments and just plain playing added up to a considerable amount of money. Counting travel costs, the junior tournaments Tiger entered cost his family about $25,000 to $30,000 a year. The Woodses weren't rich, and Tiger didn't make any money playing. They scrimped and saved and funded some of the travel with a loan. The family didn't take a non-golf holiday while Tiger was young. Earl and sometimes Kultida accompanied him to every competition on the road. Before Tiger was thirteen, Earl decided he would take early

At eight years old, weighing all of seventy-five pounds, Tiger lined up a putt at the Junior World Tournament in San Diego, California, in 1984. It was his first tournament win and was followed by dozens of other victories across the country.

retirement from his job at McDonnell Douglas. That would give him the time he needed to go with Tiger to the top junior golfing events across the country.

PERSPECTIVE

As important as golf was, it remained only part of Tiger's life as he neared junior high school. His parents insisted that he not take time from his studies to play. While he might choose not to play baseball so he could concentrate on golf, he had no choice when it came to schoolwork. Studies were first.

Besides golf, Tiger did things most other American

kids did. He played Nintendo and Ping-Pong, rode his bike around the neighborhood, and spent time fooling around with buddies. He and his friends used to play tackle football in a parking lot near his home. He was a very good runner, and when he reached junior high he joined the cross-country team for a season.

Tiger's mother practiced Buddhism, an ancient religion several hundred years older than Christianity. She passed on its beliefs to her son, emphasizing the

Buddhists pray in the Wat Phra Keo, a temple in Bangkok. Kultida, a follower of Buddhism, instilled in Tiger humility and grace under pressure—values that have served him well amid the ups and downs of his career.

need for humility and meditation as he grew. The religion proved a good balance to the worldly distractions that assaulted him.

A PERSONAL MILESTONE

Tiger got better and better as he grew. Part of his improvement came because he was growing up physically—he didn't need anyone to cut down clubs for him or to let him use a tee on every shot. Another part of his improvement came from his study of the game and his unrelenting practice.

As they grow, many boys measure themselves against their fathers. They strive to see if they are as good as their role models. When they are, they are often ready for an important rite of passage into adulthood. In Tiger's case, he had a ready-made means of measuring himself against his dad—golf.

Tiger kept getting better, knowing that someday he'd be able to beat his father. Earl was a good golfer himself. He was also very competitive. He wasn't about to give up easily. But he, too, knew that the day he lost to Tiger fair and square would eventually come.

The day came on November 28, 1987, about a month before Tiger's twelfth birthday. Father and son set out for the Long Beach navy course. Playing with some friends, Tiger and Earl were close through the first nine holes. Tiger birdied, or shot 1-under par, on the tough Number 14 to tie his dad. They stayed neck and neck for the next two holes. Then on Number 17,

Tiger managed to drop his ball with his second shot—another birdie. Earl took three shots to sink his ball.

"Daddy," Tiger said, "I'm ahead of you."

The round ended with Tiger one shot ahead of his dad. Tiger still had a long way to go before he could compete with the best golfers in the world. His dad and mom still had to ferry him around and accompany him to tournaments. But he had met an important challenge at a young age. He had beaten the man who had first taught him the game. Tiger Woods could now step out on his own.

Tiger holds the trophy in 1994 for having won his first U.S. Amateur Championship. He would set a record by also winning the event in 1995 and 1996.

Chapter **THREE**

"LET THE LEGEND GROW"

TIGER **W**OODS **TOOK A BREATH AS HE WALKED** toward the tee at the Sawgrass golf course in Ponte Vedra Beach, Florida. The eighteen-year-old was playing in the last round of the 1994 U.S. Amateur Championship. Already it had been a tough match. In the third round, he had been matched against Buddy Alexander, the golf coach of the University of Florida Gators. The contest came down to the back nine, or last nine holes. The crowd had included a few racists, including one who said rather loudly to another, "Who do you think these people are rooting for, the nigger or the Gator coach?"

Tiger had hung in there and won the third round and the next. For the final, he was matched against a

GOLF BASICS

The object of golf is very simple—using a club, hit a small ball into a small hole. Learning the basics doesn't take long. Perfecting them can take a lifetime.

Golfers score a point, or stroke, each time they hit the ball. The goal is to score the fewest number of strokes. A golfer hits the ball, waits until it stops, then hits it again until sinking it in the cup at the end of the hole. The word *hole* is used to mean both the cup and the entire playing area around and leading to the cup.

Golf courses typically have 18 holes, although they can have 9 and in some cases 27 or even 36 holes. A round of golf is usually 18 holes. A professional tournament generally consists of four rounds. Whoever scores the lowest overall total is the winner.

Players begin by teeing off, or hitting the ball from a tee at the starting area. Their goal is the cup a few hundred yards away. The cup sits on a green, a special area with very smooth grass. Gentle shots, called putts, are used to roll the ball into the hole.

Between the starting area and the green is a long fairway, which has short grass where the ball can be easily hit. Slightly higher grass known as the rough is generally located on either

friend, Trip Kuehne. Kuehne, four years older, took an early lead in the long final match. Entering afternoon play, Tiger was down by four strokes.

He knew he could come back. As Tiger walked toward the tee to start the final 18 holes, his dad took hold of him and pulled him aside.

side of the fairway. Golfers usually find it a little harder to hit a ball from the rough because of the height of the grass and nearby obstacles, such as trees.

To make things even more difficult, traps, or bunkers, sit near the green. These are areas of sand or rough earth. Hitting a ball from a bunker requires a great deal of skill. The ball must be lofted from the trap just hard enough to clear the sand but not so hard as to sail into another hazard. Pools of water and large wooded areas also make things more complicated for golfers. If a ball lands in one of these areas, the golfer must hit it out or add a penalty shot to his or her score.

The overall design of each hole—a tee, a fairway, a green—is the same from hole to hole and course to course. But the shape of individual holes varies greatly. The distance from tee to cup also varies. Each golf course presents different problems to the players.

When designers create a golf course, they consider each hole and determine how many shots a very good golfer would need to get the ball from the tee into the cup. This number is called par. Golfers can measure themselves against par on each hole. Par for each hole usually ranges from 3 to 5, depending on the size of the golf course. In most cases, expert golfers are expected to need only two putts to sink a ball once they reach the green.

"Son," Earl said, "let the legend grow."

Tiger nodded and went to address the ball. It was a great pep talk—simple and to the point. The only problem was, at first it didn't seem to work. Tiger fell five strokes back on the first six holes. But then Kuehne began to falter slightly. Tiger began to play daringly, taking do-or-die shots—and making them. Hole after hole, he fought back and tied the match at the end of the 16th hole.

The cup on the 17th green at Sawgrass lay very close to a water hazard. Most golfers attempted to place the ball on the other side, a strategy that usually cost them at least one stroke. Their logic was simple— placing the ball next to the hole from the tee was almost impossible.

Woods chose a pitching wedge and hit a soft fade into the wind. The golf ball shot high in the air. It seemed to hover there, trying to decide whether to land in the water or on the green. If it landed in the water, the match would essentially be over. Woods would have to take penalty shots and fall behind. If it landed on the green, Woods would be positioned to take a powerful lead.

The ball fell on the grass and bounced. Its roll took it within a foot and a half of the water—but it was still on the green.

"Divine intervention," said Kuehne's father after the fantastic shot that clinched the championship for his son's friend.

Top Coaches

The victory at Sawgrass made Tiger the youngest person ever to win the U.S. Amateur. Though just eighteen, he already was a polished competitor with many trophies to display. Tiger won the U.S. Junior

Amateur in 1991 at age fifteen, then again in 1992 to become the first golfer to win the event twice. A first-place finish in 1993 gave him an unprecedented three in a row. He was, by any measure, an excellent golfer.

This wasn't an accident. Tiger had taken his natural skills and honed them through practice and more practice. He had also received very good coaching. Besides Rudy Duran and his father, Tiger had advanced with the help of different coaches who worked on aspects of his game. John Anselmo, the head teaching pro at Meadowlark Golf Club in Huntington Beach, California, worked with him on his swing, after Duran left southern California for another job. By working on Woods's mechanics, Anselmo helped the athlete add power without making his drives start hooking, or curving in the air.

Tiger got even more help from one of the country's top swing coaches, Claude "Butch" Harmon. Harmon had taught one of Tiger's heroes, Greg Norman, as well as other golf superstars. Harmon went to work refining Tiger's swing, helping him get more control and accuracy in his game.

"Tiger showed me some of the shots that he could hit, and I made some suggestions to him at the time that would make him more consistent," Harmon said. "It was nothing special but I guess he liked the results that he saw." Harmon often worked over the phone or after watching videotape of Tiger. Golf reporter Tim

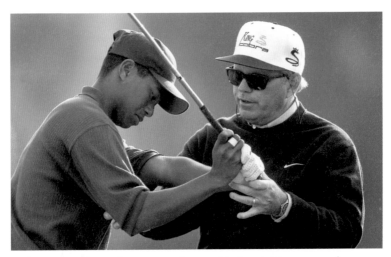

In his teens, Tiger began working with Butch Harmon, who helped solidify Tiger's swing to be a consistent and dependable weapon on the golf course.

Rosaforte said that Harmon could tell how Tiger's swing was going just by asking him the question, "Where's the ball starting?"

Harmon's ability to give Woods advice over the phone—and Tiger's ability to use it—was one of the factors that helped Woods win the Amateur Championship. After a phone call during the tournament, Tiger immediately put his coach's advice to work.

Tiger's coaches weren't all working on his mechanics. Navy captain and clinical psychologist Jay Brunza, a golfer and friend of his father's, helped him with the psychological aspects of the game. Brunza also caddied and played with him occasionally. He taught Tiger techniques for focusing and keeping the mental edge that is so important in competition. Tiger also listened to tapes on relaxation techniques as well as pep talks that helped him stay poised and confident on the course.

A RUSH OF SUCCESS

By his teen years, Tiger had already settled on his course. He knew he wanted to be a golf professional. "I want to tear it up on the [PGA] Tour," he told a reporter when he was still competing as a junior. Tiger's grades were near perfect, and he also wanted to continue his schooling. He was already thinking about what he wanted to study in college.

Tiger's high school years had rushed by in a blur. He spent an enormous amount of time playing golf—summers, vacations, weekends, and hours and hours after school. He seemed always to have a golf club in his hand, even in the living room, where Tiger would chip shots over the coffee table. He learned to be extremely accurate there. If he missed and broke any of his mom's good crystal, the consequences would be dire!

But he also studied hard and found time for fun things. He loved *The Simpsons,* a popular animated TV show, and he videotaped pro wrestling matches. He also developed a love of McDonald's and other fast food restaurants. His high school was predominantly white. Earl said Tiger grew up "surrounded by white friends."

As a freshman, Tiger made the varsity golf team at

In high school, Tiger was already amazing the golf world by winning junior amateur titles, as well as athletic awards.

Western High in Anaheim. It quickly became clear to his teammates and coach that he was something special. Besides his three U.S. Junior Amateur Championship wins, at seventeen Tiger took home the coveted Dial Award, given annually to the best high school athlete in the country.

But many, many golfers rocket to success as juniors, only to flame out as they advance to college and the higher levels of play. Tiger still had to prove himself in the long run.

COMING HOME

As he wrapped up his high school years, Tiger was in an enviable position. College coaches came to him, trying to recruit him. They offered scholarships and promised him the chance to play the sport at a very high level, with excellent coaches and well-groomed golf courses.

Tiger narrowed down his college search to two places: the University of Nevada at Las Vegas—UNLV, as it is commonly known—and Stanford University in California. Both colleges have excellent sports programs. He visited UNLV and was impressed by the golf coach as well as the excellent facilities the golf teams used.

But then he went to Stanford. Stanford's golf coach, Wally Goodwin, had been corresponding with Tiger for several years, ever since he saw a small feature on him in *Sports Illustrated*. Goodwin, like many others, had taken notice of Tiger's junior victories and realized his great potential. Many top athletes had Stanford diplomas on their walls. The college had a beautiful campus and some of the best teachers in the country. It also promoted academic excellence. Its students included some of the brightest people in the world.

"I knew I was home," Tiger told his parents when he returned from his visit.

TERRIBLE DANCER, GREAT GOLFER

As a freshman on the Stanford golf team, Tiger was treated more or less like any freshman. He accepted the "rollaway," the cot used when three teammates shared a two-bedroom hotel room. He had to put up with a dumb nickname imposed by the seniors. He became one of the guys, although an immensely talented one.

Tiger joined the fraternity Sigma Chi and there allegedly earned the nickname Dynamite for his dancing. His friends didn't intend the name to be a compliment. "It was terrible," recalled a fellow student named Jake Poe. "On the dance floor, it looked like he was blowing up a house, or pumping up a bike," added another friend and golf teammate, Eric Crum.

But if he wasn't very adept at dancing, Woods was great at golf and getting even better. In his first collegiate competition, he shot a 4-under-par 68 to win the Tucker Invitational at the University of New Mexico in Albuquerque.

Tiger had always stood out not simply because of his golf but because of his studies. At Stanford, he studied economics and met many academic achievers. A fellow freshman had already taken every math course

Hoover Tower, a symbol of Stanford University, where Tiger enrolled as a freshman in 1994

the college offered. He was tearing up math books the way Tiger tore up golf courses, something Tiger admired. Woods became an avid reader, devouring books during his off time instead of watching TV. And he found time to go to at least some of the parties that college students enjoy.

TARGET AND SYMBOL

College was not all fun, however. Once, while returning to his dorm, Woods was robbed at knifepoint. The robber smashed his jaw and took his watch and a gold chain. Fortunately, Tiger was not seriously injured. And the robber missed his wallet and something more valuable than money—a 400-year-old miniature Buddha that usually hung from the chain. Tiger wasn't wearing the family heirloom that night.

The robber called Tiger by his name, even though Woods didn't know him. Fame had shown its dark side to the young man. He was easy to single out because he was so well known.

The color of his skin also made Tiger easy to single out. Many people treated him as if he represented all African Americans. As a symbol, Tiger was sometimes criticized, by blacks as well as whites.

In October 1994, Stanford's golf team traveled to the Jerry Pate Invitational at Shoal Creek in Birmingham, Alabama. Four years earlier, the club's founder had openly admitted that African Americans weren't allowed as members. Even though a black person was later given an honorary membership, many people thought the gesture was just for show. There was still a great deal of prejudice at the club and in the local community.

Tiger and his teammates played the first two rounds. They did fairly well, with Tiger trailing the leader by three strokes with one more day of play to go.

But then, controversy erupted. Several African Americans told Coach Goodwin that Tiger shouldn't be playing at Shoal Creek. Instead, they suggested that Tiger and the rest of the team should boycott it because of its racial prejudice. And, they added, if he didn't, they would protest.

"My first concern was the safety of my team," said Goodwin later. "But we weren't about to turn around and fly back to California and not fulfill our obligation. On the very same team are a full-blooded Navajo Indian [Notah Begay] and a Japanese-American [William Yanagisawa] and a Chinese-American [Jerry Chang], and here they're picking on Tiger. It was ludicrous."

The weather helped the golfers dodge the protesters. Hard rain gave the organizers an easy excuse to say the course was under water and closed to the public. The protesters stayed outside the front gate.

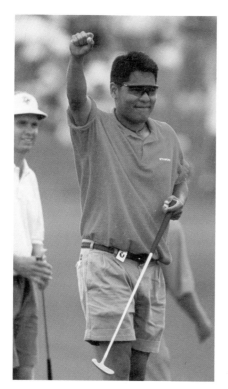

Tiger met Notah Begay, a member of the Navajo nation, while both were students at Stanford. Like Tiger, Begay turned pro and brought diversity to the nearly all-white world of golf.

Tiger shot a 5-under par and came from behind to win. It turned out to be his last first-place finish that season.

THE BIG TIME

Tiger's victory in the 1994 U.S. Amateur tournament gave him an automatic invitation to try out for the big time: the Masters Tournament at Augusta, Georgia. Though he had played in several professional events already, the Masters was far and away the most important event he had ever entered. Pros and amateurs alike regard the Masters, with its long history, as one of the sport's special competitions. Only the very best golfers in the world can walk on Augusta's fairways and greens at tourney time.

By this time, the media had carried many stories on Woods's potential and the fact that he was a young black man in a sport usually played by older white males. The press covered Tiger as if he were already a star when he came to Augusta. He attracted a large crowd when he teed off on opening day. His first shot was a beauty—a drive of 280 yards, easily clearing a difficult sand trap. He continued to play well, posting an even-par 72, which tied him for 34th in the field. He shot 72 in the next round as well, finishing high enough to stay in contention for the final rounds.

But in the third round, Tiger played poorly, posting a 5-over-par 77. That left him far off the pace. Even so, he managed a 72 on the last day of play, coming back with birdies on three of the last four holes. The showing was more than respectable, considering that Tiger was still very young.

He didn't think he had lived up to his full potential. Others agreed. Some observers seemed to relish the fact that Tiger hadn't placed with the leaders. Members of the media criticized him for not giving interviews at times and felt that his father arranged some of his actions. Earl, who could be loud and outspoken with criticism as well as praise, was called a "stage father" who pushed and controlled his son.

Through it all, Tiger struggled to keep his focus.

"You're almost there now," said his swing coach, Butch Harmon.

But almost wasn't good enough anymore.

Butch Harmon, left, Jay Brunza, center left, Earl, center right, and Tiger celebrate as the collegiate golfer wins his second amateur title in 1995. Already rumors were swirling and people were asking "When will Tiger turn pro?"

Chapter **FOUR**

TURNING PRO

AFTER THE **1995** MASTERS, TIGER WOODS WENT
back to Stanford, where he had other things to think
about—like a major exam in history. Though he still
valued academics, he was beginning to think that his
schoolwork was keeping him from reaching his full
potential as a golfer.

At the same time, the different rules governing amateur and collegiate sports chafed the budding superstar. In early October 1995, Tiger went to dinner with
one of golf's all-time greats, Arnold Palmer. Palmer,
who is rich as well as famous, paid for dinner. When
the National Collegiate Athletic Association (NCAA),
the governing board of college athletics, found out, it
decided that the free meal violated rules against

college athletes receiving special benefits. Stanford suspended Tiger from competition.

"I don't need this," Tiger told his parents angrily when he gave them the news. The suspension lasted only a day, but his parents saw the NCAA dispute as the beginning of the end of Woods's college career.

Tiger stayed on for the rest of the school year. He won a second Amateur Championship in 1995 and easily dominated on the college level during his sophomore year. Even with a heavy course load, Tiger took seven firsts. He won the NCAA Championships at the end of May 1996.

By then, sponsors on the professional tour were clamoring for him to compete in their events, as an amateur or not. The question wasn't whether he should turn pro, but when.

AMATEUR VERSUS PROFESSIONAL

In one way, the difference between amateurs and professionals is simple. Amateurs can't play for money, professionals do.

In most sports, playing for money increases the pressure of competition. A pro athlete must agree to play in a certain number of events. He or she must also follow the rules set out by the league or governing body of the sport.

In the United States, the Professional Golfers' Association (PGA) governs men's professional golf. The PGA sponsors events throughout the year. It sets rules for the sport, helps arrange for television coverage, and promotes golf in various ways. Collectively, the different events are known as the PGA Tour.

Not just anyone can compete on the PGA Tour. While there are different ways to enter individual contests, to compete on the yearlong Tour, golfers must demonstrate that they are among the best in the sport. That means they have to do well in a number of events. Only the top 125 golfers—measured by their prize money in PGA-sanctioned events—receive player's cards, making them full-fledged members of the tour.

ENDORSEMENT MONEY

Turning pro would mean that Tiger could accept prize money when he won. There are big monetary prizes for winning a PGA event. Top prizes can be more than half a million dollars. Other top scorers can earn thousands. Over the course of a year's play, top competitors can take home millions, though most players make far less.

There are other payoffs as well. Like other athletes, top golfers are also paid to give speeches and appear at certain events, like golf exhibitions and souvenir signings. Many tournaments outside the United States offer first-class golfers appearance fees, which are forbidden in the PGA. Top golfers can make $100,000 or $250,000 by agreeing to compete overseas. Someone very famous can make even more.

And then there are product endorsements.

Many companies want to use famous people to help sell their products. The companies reach agreements with stars. Sometimes, stars simply agree to use a company's equipment or other products. The firms hope fans see that their sports hero uses a certain type of glove, for example, and will look for that glove in the store. In other cases, companies hire stars to make commercials and act as representatives. They attempt to tie their product to the star's image.

To help arrange such deals, most pro athletes hire an agent. The agent represents the athlete in different business matters. By the summer of 1996, Tiger and his family had settled on the International Management Group (IMG) as his representative. Tiger and his family had met an IMG representative some years before. Earl had also worked for IMG as a scout, so it wasn't surprising that Tiger chose that company.

Even before being officially hired, IMG had lined up potential endorsement deals for Tiger. The biggest was a five-year, $40 million agreement with Nike. It was an incredible contract for an athlete who had yet to win a professional event.

SWOOSH

Nike manufactures athletic equipment, shoes, and clothes. Once Tiger turned pro, the cap and shirt he wore at golf matches always had the Nike trademark, a "swoosh," on them. He also began making commercials and advertisements for Nike.

In 1996 Tiger signed an endorsement deal with Nike, the huge sporting goods manufacturer. The Nike logo, shaped like a check mark, is on shirts and hats that Tiger wears in tournaments.

"What Michael Jordan did for basketball, [Woods] absolutely can do for golf," said the head of Nike, Phil Knight. "The world has not seen anything like what he's going to do for the sport. It's almost art. I wasn't alive to see Monet paint, but I am alive to see Tiger play golf, and that's pretty great."

Michael Jordan is one of the greatest basketball players of all time. His endorsements had helped Nike become one of the most successful athletic equipment companies. While Jordan continued to serve as the company's spokesperson, in some ways Nike had found his successor in Tiger.

Nike wanted to capitalize on Tiger's fame. But he would benefit as well. Not only did he get a large sum of money, but the commercials would also give him a great deal of exposure. The fact that a successful sports company had chosen to make him such an important spokesperson would also help his image. That would make his endorsement even more valuable in the future.

Endorsement deals have been around for a long time, but it was unusual for someone who had yet to compete as a pro to receive such a big contract. Nike was taking a risk, since something might happen to Tiger to make him look like a bad spokesperson. He might not be able to stand the pressure of turning pro and might lose a lot of events, for example.

But there were several reasons that made the deal a good move. Tiger already played well. He was already known beyond golf. And besides being a great athlete, he was a mostly soft-spoken, clean-living young man. There were no dark clouds in his past, and none were likely in his future. He didn't use drugs and didn't fool around with women. Advertisers didn't have to worry that he would be involved in a scandal that might hurt their sales.

Even more important, the media had already begun to spin a simple, positive story line about him: He was a young black man trying to integrate the top ranks of golf. Nike would use that image and even help shape it in ads.

Woods wasn't the first black golfer. He always made that clear. He also emphasized that he was Asian as well as African American, Native American, and Caucasian. Still, most people saw him as black. And most people, including golfers, associated the sport with whites. Many people—whites as well as blacks—would root for Tiger to succeed because his victories symbolized racial justice to them.

His youth also helped him. The popular image of golf was as a sport for older men. The fact that someone barely out of his teens could compete and win made that person unique in the public's eye. Any company wishing to portray itself as youthful could do so simply by using him as a spokesperson.

DECISION TIME

None of the big money deals could happen until Tiger turned pro. As the summer of 1996 wound down, he prepared for the U.S. Amateur, the championship he had won twice before. As if to prove that it was time to make his move, he won for a third straight time—something no one had ever done.

"It's time to go," he told his parents when he got back from the tournament.

A few days later in Milwaukee, Wisconsin, Tiger Woods confirmed that he planned to turn pro. He quit school, although he said he hoped to return to his studies someday. The endorsement money immediately poured in. Nike finalized its contract for five years and a total of $40 million, with a $7.5 million signing bonus. Titleist, a major manufacturer of golf

Michael Jordan and Tiger hold Nike's biggest endorsement contracts. Tiger has developed a close friendship with Jordan, not only a world-renowned basketball player but also a pretty decent golfer. They face much the same publicity barrage on the court and on the course.

balls, golf clubs, and other golfing equipment, offered him $3 million a year. That contract was soon negotiated into a five-year deal that paid him $20 million and called for him to use Titleist clubs as soon as the company could design a set for him. By the end of 1996, his endorsement fees were dwarfed only by basketball star Michael Jordan's earnings.

At first, Tiger seemed somewhat overwhelmed. "The best thing about getting all this stuff is the bags," said Tiger when he discovered that his new sponsors had sent him a few as gifts. "I'm serious. The Nike [golf] bags have so many pockets. They're awesome." His coach Butch Harmon described him as a "10-year-old dropped into the middle of Toys "R" Us."

"ARE YOU READY?"

Nike used Tiger's image in ads and commercials right away. One of the first prominent ads declared, "I shot in the 70s when I was 8. I shot in the 60s when I was 12. I won the U.S. Junior Amateur when I was 14. . . . I won the U.S. Amateur when I was 18. I played in the Masters when I was 19. I am the only man to win three consecutive U.S. Amateur titles. There are still golf courses in the United States that I cannot play because of the color of my skin. I'm told I'm not ready for you. Are you ready for me?"

People immediately objected to the line about discrimination, saying that it was incorrect. Tiger Woods could play anywhere he wanted. He was so famous that people would love to have him at their course.

Another African American on the tour pointed out that earlier African American golfers had faced real prejudice. "Every time Charlie Sifford won a tournament, they changed the rule at the Masters so he couldn't play," said Jim Thorpe, who criticized Nike, not Tiger. "With Lee Elder and Charlie, you'd hear the N-word, but I didn't have to go through it," Thorpe added.

Nike responded that the line was meant symbolically—that some blacks were still not allowed to play at courses or join clubs in the United States. The tone of the ad was aggressive and combative. While Tiger Woods is a fierce competitor on the golf course, in person he is a soft-spoken gentleman. Golf has a more gentlemanly image than many other sports, such as football or basketball. The Nike ads rubbed many in the sport the wrong way.

"We knew that Tiger turned on the thousand-watt smile whenever a TV camera was around but could be short and surly with those he didn't deem important," said John Feinstein, a sportswriter. Feinstein soon

WHAT'S IN THE BAG?

Golfers use different types of clubs, depending on where they are on a golf course. Clubs can be divided into three general categories: woods, irons, and specialty clubs like the putter.

The most numerous clubs are woods and irons. Each group has several sizes, from large to small. They are numbered according to size and shape. In both cases, the lower the number, the farther the club is expected to send a ball when hit. However, there is a tradeoff. For most golfers, the lower-numbered clubs give less loft, or height, on a shot and less accuracy.

Woods are often thought of as the long-distance clubs. They can send a ball far down a fairway. They are called woods because the head (the part of the club that hits the ball) was originally made of wood. While the heads are no longer always made of wood, the clubs' general shape and purpose remains the same. They have large, round heads with a flat surface for striking the ball. The shaft, which connects the head to the handle, is very long.

Wood sizes begin at 1 and extend to 5. The 1-wood is called a driver. The driver and the 3-wood are the most common clubs for teeing off because they can hit the ball a great distance. An average recreational male golfer would be expected to hit a became well known for his attempts to debunk what he called "the Tiger myth."

The Nike ads soon changed. And, like Michael Jordan before him, Tiger Woods became an athlete so famous he could be referred to and recognized by a single name: Tiger.

ball at least 200 yards when teeing off. Tiger Woods averages about 300 yards in competition.

Golfers need more control and loft for shorter shots on the fairway or in the rough. There, golfers generally use an iron. The heads of irons are made of metal. They have shorter shafts and their heads are more angled than woods. Like woods, the higher the number of the club, the higher a ball will go. But it won't travel as far.

Irons with low numbers—1 through 4—are called long irons because they are best used for long shots. On the other end of the spectrum are the short irons, 8 and 9, along with the pitching wedge.

The two groups of golf clubs overlap. Some golfers prefer to use a long iron instead of a wood in certain situations, and vice versa. Selecting the proper club is one of the great arts of the game.

In some situations, the right club is obvious. A special club, called a sand wedge, is used when a ball lands in a bunker or sand trap. This club is sharply angled to help lift the ball from the trap.

On the green, a putter is used. The head of this club is small and very flat. Putters allow golfers to control the direction of the ball with great precision.

The rules of golf limit golfers to carrying just fourteen clubs. The rules also govern the shape and construction of the clubs.

MOVING UP, THEN DOWN

Despite the big contracts, major advertising campaigns, and media attention, Tiger Woods still needed to prove himself. Perhaps tired by all the hoopla, he finished well down in the standings at his first pro event, in Milwaukee. Over the next few weeks, he began a slow but steady march toward higher finishes. He took fifth in the Quad City Classic and then third in the B.C. Open. After that, he needed only a few decent showings to earn his tour card.

But the stress of his new life got to him when he arrived in Pine Mountain, Georgia, for the Buick Challenge. After a practice round, he decided he was too tired to compete. He canceled and went home, missing not just the tournament but also an important awards dinner scheduled in his honor. As the top college golfer in the country the year before, he had won the Fred Haskins Award. The award would have been presented at a dinner at Pine Mountain. The dinner was canceled, and critics besieged him.

Some later pointed out that it was the first professional event Tiger had been to without his dad or his coach, Butch Harmon. But Tiger didn't use that as an excuse, admitting a few days later that he had been immature to blow off the dinner.

"I am human," he said in a *Golf World* column, "and I do make mistakes." His father said Tiger would make good on the money the sponsors had paid for the occasion. It was a low point in Tiger's early career.

A First First

Two weeks later, Tiger traveled to the Las Vegas Invitational. He was no longer tired. As the tournament went on, his focus sharpened. He shot a 64 on the last round, ending tied with Davis Love III. The two men began a playoff on the 18th hole.

"Great playing, Tiger," said Love as they got ready to shoot it out.

"Thanks, stud," said Tiger, outwardly very loose and cool.

Love walloped a good tee shot to begin. Woods took his 3-wood from the bag and followed with a good shot a short distance behind Love's. That gave Tiger the first shot, often a psychological advantage in a shoot-out. Tiger put his ball only eighteen feet from the cup.

Feeling the pressure, Love swung his 7-iron too quickly. The ball landed in a bunker just beyond the hole. Love hung tough. His shot out of the trap landed on the green, six feet from the flag.

All Tiger had to do to win was hit the middle-range putt. But it was a bit too far for him. His ball stopped two feet from the cup. He tapped it in, still confident. The best Love could do was sink his six-footer and be tied. They would go on to another hole.

Love addressed the ball well, but it slid below the cup. Tiger Woods had won his first PGA tournament.

Everyone knew it wouldn't be his last.

The golfing world would get used to seeing Tiger's pumped fist as he celebrated his victories. Here he acknowledges winning his first Masters Championship in Augusta, Georgia, in 1997, at the age of twenty-one with a record low score of 18-under par.

Chapter **FIVE**

PROMISE FULFILLED

THEY CAME PAST THE MAGNIFICENT MAGNOLIA TREES, up the lane to the clubhouse, down the long, expansive fairways. They stood patiently, along exquisite greens that shone like emeralds in the spring sun. They came in tens and hundreds and thousands, sensing something special was about to happen this warm April day in Augusta, Georgia. With golf fans the world over, they sensed that on this day, April 13, 1997, the long-promised potential of Eldrick "Tiger" Woods was about to be fulfilled.

Tiger stepped out toward the tee. Two years earlier, he had become only the fourth black in history to play at Augusta. This time, he was leading the Masters by nine strokes, an awesome edge with only one day left to play. But golf, especially at the Masters, can be a cruel heartbreaker. With so much prestige riding on a win here—with so many people looking on, with reporters everywhere—many men have crumbled on the last day.

Tiger certainly would have felt the strain if he had stopped to think about it. He'd known many triumphs, but he had also tasted failure. In the two years since playing his first Masters, Woods had undergone arthroscopic knee surgery, strained his rotator cuff, and even had a bout with food poisoning. He had won two PGA events already that year, but he longed to wear the green jacket traditionally given to the Masters' winner. He longed to stand in the long line of champions.

The world could easily have crashed on Tiger's shoulders, or at least messed up his tee shot. But Tiger Woods, just twenty-one, was so focused on his game, on where he wanted to put the ball, that he couldn't feel pressure. He couldn't feel anything, except the exquisite smack of his club against the ball.

As the crowds cheered, Tiger made Augusta his. Every element of his game—the drives from the tee, the iron shots to the green, his putting—was perfect. By the time he raised his fist in triumph on the final hole, he had shot an incredible 18-under par for the tournament, setting a scoring record with a 12-stroke lead.

He hugged his caddie, Mike "Fluff" Cowan. Then, holding his hat above his head, he walked to the edge

Earl and Tiger share an emotion-filled hug after Tiger's win at the 1997 Masters.

of the green and found the large arms of his speechless dad. Their hug celebrated the culmination of a quest that began more than twenty years before in a small suburban garage.

AN ELDER STATESMAN

Ceremonies and celebrations followed as Tiger slipped the green jacket over his red shirt with its Nike logo. Then he strode toward the putting green for another presentation. As he walked, he spotted a familiar face.

"Lee, come here," he called to Lee Elder.

He embraced Elder, who in 1975 had become the first African American to play in the Masters.

"Thanks for making this possible," Tiger told the older golfer. A tear appeared in Elder's eye.

"Augusta National had been a symbol of the old south, a place that clung to segregation," said John Feinstein, the golf writer and a historian of the Masters. Even after Elder broke the color barrier, some resentment and prejudice remained. Tiger's victory confirmed his own greatness as a golfer. It also symbolized for many African Americans that they could succeed when allowed to compete on an equal basis.

Tiger didn't break the color line. As he told Elder, an earlier generation of black golfers had paved the way for him and others. Tiger did face considerable prejudice, however. He received many hateful letters and was the subject of racist remarks by others on the tour. But his victory at the Masters answered the bigots.

As Elder put it: "After today. . . no one will even turn their head to notice when a black person walks to the first tee."

WHY SO GOOD?

Tiger Woods would never have achieved his fame or his fortune without being skillful enough to win the Masters and many other PGA events. There are several aspects to his greatness, beginning with his body and conditioning. Jack Nicklaus, whom many rank as the best golfer ever, says that the speed of Tiger's upper body as it winds against his lower body is critical on these shots.

"A friend of mine who owns professional videotape editing equipment that measures motion in thousandths of seconds compared the speed of Tiger's hips unwinding from the completion of the backswing to impact with a dozen or so other top tour players. Tiger was 20 percent faster than anyone else, and as much as 50 percent quicker than some players," said Nicklaus.

Beyond his natural assets, Tiger's mechanics are extremely good. This is largely the result of training and practice.

"He has beautiful basic fundamentals," said his coach, Butch Harmon. "He has a perfect setup, perfect posture, a perfect grip. Everything about the way he sets up for a ball is very, very good. He's always had that his whole life. That's a credit to his dad and the other people he worked with."

Harmon summed up Tiger's technique with four different points:

- Tiger has a very deliberate takeaway (beginning of his golf swing).
- Tiger uses a quick, extreme turn of his shoulders that gives him a lot of power. This translates into distance on his drives.
- His long, athletic body is very flexible as well as strong. This helps him angle his shots properly. For Harmon, one of the key flex points is Tiger's right knee, which twists elegantly on his best shots.
- Tiger uncoils his lower body very quickly, again giving him power and control.

The renowned golf coach offered one pointer for anyone watching Tiger drive: Watch his left foot. If it remains planted and balanced, the shot is likely to be a good one. Of course, Tiger himself often shows what he thinks of the shot with his reactions, jerking his hand up in triumph.

A look at Tiger's technique shows his strong, flexible body; his tightly coiled swing; and his solid footing.

Beyond his physical assets, many fellow golfers cite his mental attitude. He manages a course well, choosing the right club for the situation. He is also extremely confident and mentally tough, able to overcome distractions. Just as important, Tiger has managed to remain motivated to get better while playing at a high level.

"Like all great champions, Tiger has the ability to raise his game when he has to," said Jay Brunza, his sports psychologist. "He's not going to burn out because he plays for his own joy and passion."

Pro golfer Jay Haas had a different insight after playing a tournament round with Tiger when the star did poorly. "What struck me about Tiger that day was, as angry as he was walking to the eighth tee, he didn't blow up and he didn't give up," Haas said. "The mark of a champion isn't how you play when everything is going right. It's how you play when you're struggling. He showed me something that day."

"As a golfer, he has tremendous ability, and the great thing is, he is still learning," says retired golf great Byron Nelson. "As well as he's been playing, he realizes to himself that he can play better. It's a trait all the great champions have."

TAILING OFF

Soon after Tiger's victory at the Masters, Earl went into the hospital for surgery. Tiger worried about his father. "There are more important things in life than golf," he said while Earl was in the hospital, cutting short a news conference. "I love my dad to death, and I'm going to see him right now."

Earl recovered, but Tiger and his family then faced a sad surprise. They discovered that the man Tiger had been named after, Vuong Dang Phong, had died many years before.

The Vietnam War had ended, with Communist North Vietnam taking over South Vietnam. "Tiger One," as Earl and Tiger called Colonel Phong, had been captured by the victors and had been put in a prison because he had fought against them. An enterprising reporter named Tom Callahan tracked down Phong's family in Vietnam and the United States, only to discover that Colonel Phong had been dead for more than twenty years.

"The effect of finding out about his death was stronger than I can explain," said Tiger. "From all I've heard, the three of us are alike. I'm more hot-tempered than my father is now. But he used to be like me—and so was Tiger One."

As Tiger matured, his ties to his father and mother remained strong. Tiger and his dad sometimes had heated arguments, especially when Earl thought Tiger hadn't played up to his potential. But they remained close. Earl and Kultida, however, began living separately even though they remained married. Earl said that they still loved each other, and they were often seen together at Tiger's tournaments.

A Tiger Slump

Tiger won the GTE Byron Nelson Classic and the Motorola Western Open after taking the Masters. Overall, 1997 was a fantastic year, propelling him to a number one ranking in the sport by mid-June. At twenty-one, he was the youngest golfer ever to grab that PGA honor.

But he also had a few disappointing shows as the year went on. Though he didn't realize it, he was starting a slump that would carry into 1998. His second full year as a pro would frustrate and disappoint him and his fans.

Tiger smiles beside legendary golfer Byron Nelson, whose tournament Tiger won in 1997.

While Tiger had great success in most of 1997, he experienced a lot of inconsistency in 1998, particularly with his putting. Nevertheless, he had a good run at the Mercedes Championships in Carlsbad, California.

Chapter **SIX**

THE YEAR(S)
OF THE TIGER

TIGER STOOD OVER THE BALL, HIS LONG, LANKY frame set like a pendulum. He was at the edge of the green. The hole lay a good distance away. He needed to sink the ball to start gaining ground on the leaders. His ankle was sore, and he was very tired. But somehow he relaxed, his mind shifting into the familiar, perfect zone. His putt began almost imperceptibly as his weight shifted ever so slightly. His arms and the club swung gently, well-oiled parts in the works of a mammoth clock. The putter head smacked the ball. It rolled along the green, riding a gentle lip on the surface, then sliding down toward the cup, sliding and sliding, as if pulled by a magnet.

Except that it missed.

Not by much, but enough for one more frustration in a tournament of frustrations. The 1997 Bell Canadian Open had turned into a disaster. Just two weeks after taking third in the NEC World Series of Golf, Tiger failed to make the cut in a major PGA event for the first time since he had turned pro.

Tiger rebounded and started 1998 with strong showings at the Mercedes Championship, the Buick Invitational, and the Nissan Open, all major events where

Frustration showed on Tiger's face as he saw his tournament play become erratic in 1998.

he ranked in the top three. But as the year went on, Tiger Woods experienced a phenomenon common to all great golfers—to everyone, in fact. He was less than perfect every time out.

No one has a perfect day every day. Still, since he was Tiger Woods, people expected him to be, if not perfect, at least very, very good. If everyone said he was the best golfer to come along in a generation, shouldn't he win every tournament? When he didn't, golf journalists and other observers began talking about a slump.

Some statistics backed them up. In 1998 Tiger's putting slipped noticeably. He had ranked 60th on the tour in 1997, and he slipped to 147th. On the other hand, he was still driving the ball a great distance. His driving accuracy slipped a little, but he'd never been ranked among the most accurate drivers. And he had won the fourth highest amount of money on the Tour in 1998. Money earnings were a rough approximation of his overall ranking.

Tiger believed he got better in 1998. "I think my ball flight's improved," he said. "I'm able to play in conditions I've never been able to play before."

Rather than a slump, perhaps 1998 should have been labeled a year of inconsistency. Tiger sometimes played extremely well, sometimes played very well, a few times played only average, and once or twice played poorly. Only when measured on a very extreme scale of excellence could that be considered a slump.

HYPER CRITICISM

People measured Tiger on a very extreme scale of excellence for several reasons. One was his natural ability. As he had showed at the Masters in 1997, he had the potential to be an extremely good golfer. Since he was so young, his career could take him to the very top of the profession. Many fans wanted this to happen. Rather than measuring Woods against the other players on the Tour, they compared him to people like Jack Nicklaus or Arnold Palmer, two of the greatest golfers ever to swing a club.

Tiger's image also put him under a spotlight. Many journalists and others believed that because he made so much money, he should be held to a higher standard. In a way, they wanted him to earn that money every time he stepped on the golf course—or anywhere else. They criticized Woods for many things that ordinary people would never be knocked for doing.

For example, after his win at Augusta, Tiger was invited at the last minute to a ceremony honoring Jackie Robinson. An African American, Robinson had broken the color barrier in professional baseball and set a standard for society, as well as for athletes. Many people thought the latest athlete to break barriers should be on hand for the celebration. Even the president of the United States would be attending. But Woods had other plans for the day of the celebration. Nonetheless, he was strongly criticized for not attending. His motives, and even his father's political preferences, were questioned. When he pointed out that he was invited at the last minute and only because he had won the Masters, he was criticized again.

After a bad round at the U.S. Open in 1997, he skipped the news conference and walked to his car. Tiger was so angry that he smashed his Walkman on the dashboard and then looked up to see a reporter. He answered her questions quickly, hardly hiding his anger at how poorly he had played. Later, he apologized, explaining that he really didn't understand he was expected to answer questions when he wasn't leading the tournament.

Tiger worked harder to control his anger, but like nearly all golfers, he could be emotional when he didn't do well. Public relations specialists helped him polish his image as being above the fray, always polite if a little distant. Some players on the tour found him a little cold. Others said he was warm and even outgoing. All said he was extremely competitive and self-assured. Tiger clearly worked hard not only to improve his game but also to protect his public image. Things that didn't fit with that image—like telling dirty jokes or using foul language—he worked to minimize, or at least keep from public view.

Tiger Woods could make millions and millions of dollars but, in exchange, people wanted to view him as a symbol. If he didn't live up to their expectation of that symbol, he would be criticized—no matter what he did on the golf course.

The media were never far away in 1998, when Tiger kept up a heavy schedule of endorsement appearances, as well as playing many tournaments.

Of course, if he didn't do well on the golf course, the criticism increased tremendously.

"I FINALLY GOT IT"

The endorsement and appearance deals that brought Tiger considerable wealth obligated him to a long, grueling string of appointments. He traveled with a small group of assistants and others who attended to many minor details. He also acquired a private plane to make it easier to keep on schedule. Still, the schedule ground him down and often left him tired. But when his dad complained about the tight schedule Tiger was trying to keep, Tiger just smiled. "You know me," he said. He had been an overachiever since childhood, and he wasn't about to change his ways.

Tiger bought a townhouse in Isleworth, a neighborhood in Orlando, Florida. The townhouse cost about half a million dollars, and Tiger spent another $250,000 decorating it. But the best thing about his new house was that it was right next to a driving range. He could practice or relax without much hassle. Typically, Tiger competed in major tournaments every other week, resting during the off week. He told visitors to his website that he liked to play with his computer in his down time and even invested on-line.

Tiger remained close to both of his parents, even though they were living separately. Despite occasional

WHAT IF. . . .

Judging from his fan club's website, many people wonder what Tiger would be doing if he didn't play golf.

His answer? Play golf.

For fun, that is. Woods studied economics at Stanford University. He said he'd probably be in business if he hadn't been able to make it as a pro golfer. Instead of playing golf for a living, he would be doing it in his free time.

Woods never obtained his college degree. But he has said several times that he hopes to finish his studies and receive his diploma.

The official fan site, produced by CBS Sportsline, is located on the Internet at <http://www.clubtiger.com>. Users must be older than thirteen and must register.

disagreements, Tiger's parents were visible and vocal supporters of their son.

Beyond the money, the appearances, the schedules, the parties, and the media attention, there was one great truth: Tiger Woods loves to play golf. As hard as practice could be, it was still fun. Tiger went to work with Coach Harmon, breaking down his swing and analyzing it. Tiger wanted to improve his accuracy without losing his great power. But as many athletes know, analyzing something can hamper performance. By breaking down the components of his swing, something that once seemed natural suddenly became something he had to think about.

As the 1999 tour began, Tiger's swing became something he didn't have to think about so much. His accuracy improved so that his drives stayed on the fairway more often, in good position for him to reach the green. Statistically, the difference was small, but the effect was huge.

"I finally got it," he told his coach. "It all starts to feel natural to me."

His putting suddenly became deadeye accurate. As 1999 continued, the slump ended with a bang.

Starting with the Buick Invitational, Tiger won eight major events on the PGA Tour in 1999. He took a second and a third, giving him top finishes in more than half of the major tournaments. Eighteen times, he landed in the top 25, and sixteen times he was in the top 10. He made every cut. He won $6,616,585, far more than anyone else on the tour. It was the most dominating year a golfer had had since Jack Nicklaus's prime. But it was just the warmup for 2000.

TEAM TIGER . . . AND A GIRLFRIEND

As 1999 drew to a close and Tiger got ready for the 2000 season, he made several changes to "Team Tiger," the group of coaches and professional managers around him. Observers said the changes were part of his maturing process. At twenty-four, he felt surer of himself and took more control of his decisions. His new agent, Mark Steinberg, was friendlier. His new caddie, Steve Williams, seemed more low-key than his previous one. Some observers viewed the changes as a sign that Tiger was becoming his own man, moving away from the advisers his father had first helped him select. The changes may have reflected a more laid-back approach, the mark of a self-assured, maturing athlete. But Tiger himself didn't make a big deal about them and played down the change in caddies especially.

Woods also began seeing a steady girlfriend, a law student at Pepperdine University named Joanna Jagoda. She was good looking and intelligent. "Friends said she brought a sense of normalcy to his life," reported sportswriter Tim Rosaforte. "I'm always impressed by her character, her poise and her sense of perspective despite the ferocious hurricane that surrounds her boyfriend," said Golf Channel personality Peter Kessler.

Girlfriend Joanna Jagoda began appearing at Tiger's tournaments in 1998.

With his new team in place, the young superstar set out to see if he could go 1999 one better.

GRAND SLAM

Since golf became a big-time professional sport, fans and pros have focused on four major events: the Masters, the U.S. Open Championship, the British Open Championship, and the PGA Championship. These four tournaments consistently offer the most competitive and difficult matches in the sport. Collectively, the four tournaments have become known as the "grand slam." To win all four in the same year has become a legendary goal, approachable by only the best of the very best. Only one professional golfer had ever taken three of the four—Ben Hogan, who because of scheduling difficulties couldn't attend the British Open in 1953. Since then, the closest anyone had come to taking a grand slam was Jack Nicklaus in 1975. He won the first event, the Masters, and the last, the PGA Championship. He lost the other two tournaments by a grand total of three strokes.

Like every other pro golfer, Tiger regarded the grand slam as the greatest achievement possible. Even a career grand slam, or winning all four events during his career instead of in one year, would be a remarkable achievement. But hampered by a poor (for him) first round, Tiger placed fifth at the 2000 Masters. His game caught fire that spring, however, and he won the U.S. Open and then the historic British Open Championship with impressive performances. So while the "official" grand slam was out of the question when he went to the PGA Championship that August, golf fans the world over were watching him. If he took three out of four events, he would have done what Jack Nicklaus had failed to do a generation before. The comparisons with "the Golden Bear," as Nicklaus was often called, would take on more meaning.

Not only that—Nicklaus, a noted golf course architect, had designed the Valhalla Golf Course in New York where the tournament would be held. And to increase the interest for fans, he was playing there, hosting the event. Woods was paired with Nicklaus for the first two rounds.

On the first day, Tiger shot a sizzling 66, which tied him for the lead with Scott Dunlap. After the second day, Tiger had a two-day score of 133, one stroke over Dunlap. Nicklaus, long past his prime, played well but eventually fell back. Nicklaus was at 148, which wasn't enough to make the cut.

No one knew until the final two rounds began that Woods's real competition would come from Bob May. Until then, hardly anyone outside of the tour knew May. A few years older than Tiger, he had grown up not far from the Woods family in California. Tiger had broken many of May's amateur records. May's promise as a young man hadn't seemed to translate as a pro— until Valhalla.

May shot a 66 on the third round to finish one stroke behind Woods. On the last round, he again stroked a 66, one better than Woods, which left them tied.

SHOOT-OUT AT VALHALLA

A three-hole playoff began at Number 16. The gallery, or crowd of fans, was going wild.

"Is this what you get every week?" May asked Woods as the noise became overwhelming.

At the PGA Championship at Valhalla in 2000, Tiger willed the ball into the hole for a birdie.

"You got it," said Tiger.

Tiger birdied the hole, thanks to an incredible 7-iron shot that sailed more than 170 yards to the green. A twenty-foot putt gave him a one-shot lead. He held it on the next hole, Number 17. That gave him a single stroke advantage as they teed up for the last hole.

Woods's drive went wildly left, hit a golf cart, bounced into trees, and then somehow found a decent lie in the grass. But two shots later, he ended up in a bunker.

May, meanwhile, managed to find the green on his third shot. His ball lay closer to the cup than Tiger's. May could easily two-putt the hole. Unless Tiger made a phenomenal shot from the trap, May could win this hole and force a sudden-death playoff.

All eyes turned to Woods as he walked toward the deep sand trap. Tiger's entire body disappeared from view as he prepared to swing. Suddenly, the ball sailed out of the bunker and flew toward the hole. It stopped a bare eighteen inches away from the cup.

Woods tapped it in and waited.

May's ball lay sixty feet from the pin. He needed to make an incredibly long putt to tie. It would be difficult, but not impossible.

He took a breath and swung. The ball rolled along perfectly, closer, closer, closer—then it stopped at the lip of the cup.

Tiger Woods had won three out of four events in the Grand Slam. He had had golf's best season ever, by any measure.

Tiger's PGA Championship win in 2000 started off a record-breaking year that later was called a "Tiger Slam."

Chapter **SEVEN**

TIGER SLAM

TIGER **W**OODS **FINISHED THE PRACTICE ROUND AT** Pebble Beach on January 31, 2001. Turning to head for the clubhouse, he found himself in the middle of a surging group of fans looking for his autograph. The next thing he knew, he had twisted his knee.

"I was walking off the green," he told reporters later. "A lot of fans just kind of got on top of me. One guy ran right in front, and I stepped on his ankle. My weight going forward, his weight coming toward me, just hyperextended my knee."

A physical therapist in the fitness trailer at the course diagnosed the injury as a sprained ligament. Woods decided to play in the tourney, even though he was limping afterward and probably in considerable pain. He ended in 13th place, though he didn't blame the injury or the autograph hound for his showing. But the incident showed that even someone with exceptional talent and skill, a tough mental attitude, and a fierce competitive streak has to face the unexpected.

A DRY SPELL

Tiger ran into his fan during the middle of a dry spell. After he won the three majors in 2000, fans, commentators, and other golfers began debating whether Tiger could take the 2001 Masters. And, they wondered, would that unprecedented streak amount to a grand slam? Some said it wouldn't. They thought all four events had to be won in the same calendar year. Others noted that the idea of a slam was to hold all the championships at the same time. Regardless, a fourth major title in a row would rank among the greatest sports achievements of all time.

For the first two months of 2001, there seemed little reason to debate. In January and February, Tiger finished no higher than fourth in any tournament. His putting was way off. From ranking as the second-best putter on the tour in 2000, he dropped to 140th. Even his drives weren't carrying as far as they had the previous summer.

But then came the Bay Hill Invitational in March. With a bounce off a spectator at the final hole, Tiger beat Phil Mickelson by a stroke to end his victory drought. Two weeks later, Woods made it two straight

Tiger was on a winning streak in 2000 and kept up the pace by winning the Players Championship in Ponte Vedra Beach, Florida, in March 2001.

with a victory at the Players Championship in Ponte Vedra Beach, Florida. His 26th career win showed everyone he was back in top form. He had set the stage for the Masters.

MASTER PRESSURE

Hype and excitement mixed as the 2001 Masters began in the first week of April. Tiger struggled in the first round. The headlines belonged to Chris DiMarco, an unknown rookie from Long Island, New York. Trying to win the first Masters he had ever entered, DiMarco blistered the course on opening day with a 7-under par 65. Tiger's 70 left him far back in the pack.

Day two went a bit better for Woods. He logged a 66 and chugged into second place. But DiMarco stayed hot and on top at 10-under par. Meanwhile, Mickelson led a pack of other top players vying for the lead.

Tiger and DiMarco played together on Saturday in the third round. The underdog rookie hung tough through the front nine, but Woods charged ahead relentlessly. He birdied the 13th hole, birdied the 14th, and then made a light chip on the 15th to set up his third straight birdie. Those three holes wilted DiMarco and pushed Tiger into the lead.

Still, no one was giving up just yet. Mickelson made his move, pulling into second place. One shot back, he was ready for a showdown with the man who had edged him out at Bay Hill a month before. Mickelson, a gifted golfer himself, had been chasing Tiger his whole career.

"I desperately want this," Mickelson told a reporter for the Associated Press. He wanted to win the Masters and didn't mind that he would have to beat Woods to do it. "I've been preparing not just this past year, not just the past 10 years, but since I was a kid picking up balls at a driving range."

DiMarco and Mark Calcavecchia were two strokes back. Just behind them were David Duval and Ernie Els, fierce competitors capable of making up the three-stroke deficit.

"Tiger being Tiger, he's not going to back down," said Els. "But there's a lot of talent on that leaderboard."

"We'll be clawing together all day," predicted DiMarco. The prediction proved true.

FOR THE SLAM

A light breeze cooled the mammoth crowd as Tiger approached the first tee Sunday afternoon. The packed gallery and millions of television viewers held their breath as he sent a long drive down the fairway. The ball exploded off his club head, as if powered by the nervous tension in the air. But then it veered left, landing in the rough. Tiger bogeyed the hole, immediately losing his advantage.

He got back on his game through the first nine holes, battling head to head with Mickelson. Duval, playing ahead of the two leaders, surged into a tie on the back nine. Woods kept at it, finally pushing out to a two-stroke lead after 14. Roughly half an hour's worth of golf separated him from history.

Then, Tiger blew an easy three-foot putt on Number 15. Mickelson pulled to within one. Woods seemed to sag a bit on hole 16, barely managing par. But the pressure affected Mickelson as well. His tee shot careened right, forcing a difficult putt that led to a bogey on the hole, restoring Tiger's two-shot advantage. And Duval stumbled as well, missing putts on the last two holes that might have locked up an advantage. He went off the course one behind Woods. Only Tiger's miscues would give him a victory.

As Woods approached the tee for his final hole, his

entire focus settled on the small dappled ball before him. He swung and sent a monster drive down the fairway toward the hole—and into a bunker.

The crowd fell silent. Tiger's caddie, Steve Williams, handed him a wedge, exchanging a word and a glance. Woods stared at the ball. Finally, he swung. Seventy-five yards later, the ball rolled to a halt 18 feet from the hole. Eighteen feet. He'd missed easier putts. Every outstanding golfer had. The Masters has a history of breaking hearts with errant rolls a few feet, even a few inches, from victory.

Woods ignored the history. He ignored the crowd. He ignored everything but the ball. As soon as he swung, the ball hopped ahead, ducked slightly to the side, then back, back, back, and into the hole.

Vijay Singh, winner of the 2000 Masters, helps Tiger don the green jacket after Tiger won his second Masters in April 2001.

Tiger Woods had made his own history. Commentators stopped debating whether his achievement was a grand slam or not. Instead, they had found a new name for it: The Tiger Slam.

As the ball nestled into the bottom of the hole, Tiger Woods froze on the green. He stared into space, and then, for the first time in his professional career, put his hand to his face and cried as the cameras rolled.

How Great?

When Tiger was nineteen, Earl was criticized for predicting his son would win "14 major championships." Rather than seeming outlandish, the prediction now seems far too conservative.

Jack Nicklaus won two U.S. Amateur Championships, six Masters, four U.S. Opens, three British Opens, and five PGA Championships. In the 1960s, his golden hair and easy smile—along with his masterful game—made him famous well beyond golf. In a way, he was an earlier generation's Tiger Woods.

Can Woods do as well as Nicklaus did? "Tiger clearly possesses all of the physical tools and seemingly the mental qualities to rewrite the record books," said Nicklaus, "which leaves only the questions of desire and physical well-being. He did get awfully rich awfully fast once he turned pro, but if he can put that aside . . . to retain his competitive hunger, along with handling fame, his long-term impact on the game could be awesome."

THE GOLDEN BEAR

J ack Nicklaus *(below, left)* began playing golf when he was six, although he says the golf bug didn't bite him until about 1957, when he was seventeen. Two years later, he was the top amateur golfer in the country, the youngest in forty years to earn that honor. By the time he turned pro in 1962, it was clear that Nicklaus had the potential to be one of the best players ever. Forty years later, he is generally considered the greatest of all time.

Nicklaus won two U.S. Amateur Championships, six Masters, four U.S. Opens, three British Opens, and five PGA Championships. Nicknamed the Golden Bear because of his blond hair and athletic frame, he won nearly one hundred tournaments around the world in his prime. He is well known as an architect and designer of golf courses, as well as one of the sport's ambassadors. Any newcomer with promise—including Tiger Woods—is inevitably compared to him.

So what does Nicklaus think of Woods?

"I got a close-up view of Tiger Woods's capabilities when Arnie [Arnold Palmer] and I played a practice round with him at the 1996 Masters," writes Nicklaus in his autobiography *Jack Nicklaus: My Story*. "Afterward I told the media that he was not only the most fundamentally sound golfer I'd ever seen but an exceptionally composed individual for his years, as well as a most pleasant and appealing young man."

Nicklaus believes Tiger could win more Masters than he did.

RICHES

By 2001 Tiger was the most dominating golfer of his time. And he was very rich. Organizers of golf tournaments outside the United States had increased to $2 million the fee they were willing to pay Tiger to appear. Woods had signed a new endorsement contract with Nike worth an estimated $100 million.

Tiger's success has helped golf in many ways. Television audiences increase when he is part of an event, making it possible to hike advertising rates and the winners' fees. Attendance at PGA events has also increased in the years since he went pro, as have endorsement deals for other golfers. A survey by *Golf World* magazine estimated that the top seventy-five players on the PGA Tour made $1 million or more each, between winners' fees and endorsement income.

Not all of this success was because of Tiger Woods, of course. Advertisers note that many golf fans are older males who are hard to reach except through the sport. "Golf has a pretty ripe audience," said Tom Jump, who coordinates advertising for Buick. "It's educated, affluent, and in the 35- to 50-year-old range. Golf has helped us appeal to a wider audience."

But Woods definitely has had a major impact. In 2000, Tiger and the PGA quarreled when the PGA used his image to advertise events he wasn't attending. The disagreement was quickly settled. Still, it was clear that he can have an influential part in golf's future if he wants it.

Woods is so famous that nearly anything he does becomes news—even dyeing his hair blond or shaving it off, as he did in early 2001. He won new respect for golf by being named athlete of the year in 1997, 1999, and 2000 by the Associated Press. *Forbes* ranked him number two on its 2001 list of most powerful celebrities. Commentator Bob Costas said Tiger symbolizes not just golf or athletics, but an entire era.

"The rarest of all sports heroes are those who transcend sports and define the spirit of their times. Think of Babe Ruth in the '20s, Muhammad Ali in the '60s, Michael Jordan in the '90s," said Costas. "Will Tiger ultimately be regarded as the greatest of them all? It's still too early to say. But the legend is growing."

In 2001, stylishly dressed in a tux, Tiger accepted one of four ESPY awards (from the sports network ESPN) given him that year. The four citations—for Male Athlete of the Year, Pro Golfer of the Year, Championship Performance, and Come From Behind Performance—broke the record of three awards he once shared with Michael Jordan.

TIGER'S CAREER HIGHLIGHTS...SO FAR

n a career with so many high points, it's hard to come up with a definitive list. Here's a sampling of how Tiger became a household name.

1984: won his first of six Optimist International Junior Tournaments

1991–1993: won U.S. Junior Amateur Championships back to back, the youngest champion ever

1994–1996: won U.S. Amateur Championships back to back, the youngest champion ever

1996: turned pro in August and promptly won two events; named *Sports Illustrated* Sportsman of the Year

1997: won first Masters by a record 12 strokes; set a record by winning five PGA events in first sixteen tournaments; ranked number one for the first time, the youngest to ever win the honor; named Male Athlete of the Year by the Associated Press and PGA Player of the Year

1998: had an "off" year, winning only three golf events; fourth on the money list with more than $1.8 million yearly income

1999: won eight major events on the PGA Tour and garnered more than $6.6 million; again voted Male Athlete of the Year by the Associated Press and PGA Player of the Year

2000: won three of four Grand Slam majors: the U.S. Open, the British Open, and the PGA Championship; named Male Athlete of the Year by Associated Press for the third time

2001: won his second Masters; along with his three other slam events in 2000, is the first golfer to be reigning champion of all four majors simultaneously

SOURCES

7   John Strege, *Tiger* (New York: Broadway Books, 1997), 11.
11 Earl Woods with Fred Mitchell, *Playing Through* (New York: HarperCollins, 1998), 36.*
11 Ibid., 37.
12 Strege, 8.
15 E. Woods, *Playing Through*, 61.
16 Tim Rosaforte, *Tiger Woods—The Makings of a Champion* (New York: St. Martin's Press, 1997), 17.
22 E. Woods, *Playing Through*, 102.
24 "Woods Doesn't Want to Be Called African-American," Associated Press, April 22, 1997, Archived at <www.texnews.com/tiger/race042297.html> (n.d.).
24 Tiger Woods statement, n.d., <www.cbs.sportsline.com/u/fans/celebrity/tiger/about/quotes.html> (n.d.).
24 Strege, 16.
25 Tiger Woods, foreword to *Training a Tiger*, by Earl Woods with Pete McDaniel (New York: HarperCollins, 1997), xi.
25 E. Woods, *Playing Through*, 104.
27 E. Woods, *Training a Tiger*, 160.
27 Rosaforte, 23.
31 E. Woods, *Playing Through*, 88.**
33 Strege, 71.
35 Ibid., 75.
36 Ibid., 76.
37 Rosaforte, 82.
38 Ibid.

*There are several ways to spell Phong's name. This book uses the spelling that was adopted after the deceased South Vietnamese colonel's family was located.

**Note that Earl's account differs slightly from the actual recorded scorecard of the event, which this book relies on for its description.

39 Ibid., ix.
39 E. Woods, *Playing Through*, 15.
42 Ibid., 116.
42 Strege, 82.
42 Ibid., 82.
44–45 Ibid., 89.
47 Ibid., 107.
50 Ibid., 157.
53 Rosaforte, 165.
55 Ibid., 169.
56 Strege, 191.
56 Ibid.
57 Ibid., 195.
57 Rosaforte, 183.
58 John Feinstein, *The First Coming—Tiger Woods: Master or Martyr* (New York: The Library of Contemporary Thought, Ballantine Publishing Group, 1998), 45.
60 Strege, 205.
61 Rosaforte, 5.
65 Tim Rosaforte, *Raising the Bar* (New York: Thomas Dunne Books, St. Martin's Press, 2000), 129.
65 Ibid.
65 John Feinstein, *The Majors* (New York: Little, Brown & Company, 1999), 22.
66 Rosaforte, *Raising the Bar*, 129.
66 Jack Nicklaus with Ken Bowden, *Jack Nicklaus: My Story* (New York: Simon & Schuster, 1997), 414.
67 *Tiger Woods: Heart of a Champion*, produced by Intersport Inc., 40 minutes, 2000, videocassette.
69 Jay Brunza, quoted at <www.cbs.sportsline.com/u/fans/celebrity/tiger/about/quotes.html/> accessed via <Frontiernet.net> (March 2, 2001).
69 Feinstein, *The Majors*, 149.
69 Rosaforte, *Raising the Bar*, xi.
69–70 Rosaforte, *The Makings of a Champion*, 235.
70 "Real Tiger Died in Vietnam Camp," Associated Press, September 14, 1997.
70 Ibid.
75 Rosaforte, *Raising the Bar*, 140.

78 E. Woods, *Playing Through,* 191.

80 Rosaforte, *Raising the Bar,* 140.

81 Ibid., 180.

81 Ibid.

84–85 Howard Richman, "Woods wins PGA Championship in playoff with May," Knight Ridder Newspapers wire service, August 21, 2000, Archived at <www.texnews.com/tiger/winn0821.html> (n.d.).

87 Clifton Brown, "Woods Injures Knee After Collision With a Fan," *New York Times,* February 1, 2001.

90 Jim Litke, "Mickelson to Face Major Crossroads in Final Round," Associated Press, April 7, 2001.

90 Doug Ferguson, "Woods Gives Himself Chance to Rewrite History Once Again," Associated Press, April 7, 2001.

91 Tim Dahlberg, "Pars Don't Help DiMarco Remain on Top of Leaderboard," Associated Press, April 7, 2001.

93 Rosaforte, *The Makings of a Champion,* 137.

93 Nicklaus, 414.

94 Ibid.

95 "Report: Golf Endorsements Reach $400 Million," Associated Press, February 7, 2001.

96 Joe Garner, Bob Costas, et al, *And the Fans Roared: The Sports Broadcasts That Kept Us on the Edge of Our Seats,* Naperville, IL: Sourcebooks, Inc., 2000, compact disc.

SELECTED BIBLIOGRAPHY

BOOKS

Feinstein, John. *The First Coming—Tiger Woods: Master or Martyr?* New York: Ballantine Publishing Company, 1998.
———. *The Majors.* New York: Little, Brown & Company, 1999.
Garner, Joe, and Bob Costas, et al. *And the Fans Roared: The Sports Broadcasts That Kept Us on the Edge of Our Seats.* Naperville, IL: Sourcebooks, Inc., 2000. Compact disc.
Graffis, Herb. *The PGA.* New York: Thomas Y. Crowell Company, 1975.
Nicklaus, Jack, with Ken Bowden. *Jack Nicklaus: My Story.* New York: Simon & Schuster, 1997.
Rosaforte, Tim. *Raising the Bar.* New York: St. Martin's Press, 2000.
———. *Tiger Woods: The Makings of a Champion.* New York: St. Martin's Press, 1997.
Sinnette, Calvin H. *Forbidden Fairways: A History of African Americans and the Game of Golf.* Chelsea, MI: Sleeping Bear Press, 1998.
Strege, John. *Tiger.* New York: Broadway Books, 1997.
Wiren, Gary. *The PGA Manual of Golf.* New York: MacMillan Publishing Company, 1991.
Woods, Earl, with Pete McDaniel. *Training a Tiger.* New York: HarperCollins, 1997.
Woods, Earl, with Fred Mitchell. *Playing Through.* New York: HarperCollins, 1998.
Woods, Earl, with Shari Lesser Wenk and the Tiger Woods Foundation. *Start Something.* New York: Simon & Schuster, 2000.

MAGAZINES AND NEWSPAPER ARTICLES

Anderson, Dave. "Why Woods Hasn't Won: His Putting."*New York Times,* February 7, 2001.
Barrett, David. "2000 Year in Review." *Golf Magazine,* January 2001.

Brown, Clifton. "Gogel Sets Poppy Hills Mark and Leaves Past Behind." *New York Times,* February 3, 2001.

——. "For Love, Fast Start Means Bigger Finish." *New York Times,* February 5, 2001.

——. "At Pebble Beach, Singh Seeks His Day After Two Close Calls." *New York Times,* February 4, 2001.

——. "Woods Injures Knee After Collision With a Fan." *New York Times,* February 1, 2001.

Dahlbert, Tim. "Only Question for Woods May Be How He Wins Majors." Associated Press, August 21, 2000. Archived at <www.texnews.com/tiger/how0821.html>. (n.d.).

Ebert, Jon. "Tiger Doesn't Make Great Golf Courses Obsolete." Scripps Howard News Service. April 29, 1997. Archived at <www.texnews.com/tiger/obso042997.html>. (n.d.).

Ferguson, Doug. "Tiger Gets a Fight, but Wins PGA." Associated Press. August 21, 2000. Archived at <www.texnews.com/tiger/fight0821.html>. (n.d.).

Gola, Hank. "Epic Victory for Woods." *New York Daily News,* August 21, 2000.

Juliano, Joe. "Tiger Woods Wins Masters in Memorable Fashion." Knight-Ridder News Service. April 14, 1997. Archived at <www.texnews.com/tiger/enor041497.html>. (n.d.).

Posanski, Joe. "Woods Gives Us a Closer Look." Knight Ridder News Service. August 21, 2000. Archived at <www.texnews.com/tiger/look0821.html>. (n.d.).

Reagan, Danny. "The Impact Tiger Is Going to Make." *Abilene Reporter-News.* April 26, 1997. Archived at <www.texnews.com/tiger/dr042697.html>. (n.d.).

Richman, Howard. "Woods Wins PGA Championship in Playoff with May." Knight Ridder News Service. August 21, 2000. Archived at <www.texnews.com/tiger/winn0821.html.>. (n.d.).

"Seen & Heard." *Golf Magazine,* January 2001.

Sherman, Ed. "Tiger Woods Plays Golf with Michael Jordan, Tapes Oprah Winfrey Show." *Chicago Tribune.* April 22, 1997. Archived at <www.texnews.com/tiger/mike042297.html>. (n.d.).

Timms, Ed, and Thomas G. Watts. "Multiracial Issues for Others Raised with Hoopla Surrounding Tiger Woods." *Dallas Morning News.* April 21, 1997. Archived at <www.texnews.com/tiger/multi042197>. (n.d.).

Townsend, Brad. "After Masters Win, Some Wonder if Woods Can Hit the Grand Slam." *Dallas Morning News.* April 17, 1997. Archived at <www.texnews.com/tiger/slam041797.html>. (n.d.).

"Woods Doesn't Want to Be Called African-American." Associated Press. April 22, 1997. Archived at <www.texnews.com/tiger/race042297.html>. (n.d.).

VIDEO

Tiger Woods: Heart of a Champion. Produced by Intersport, Inc. 40 minutes. 2000.

WEBSITES

<http://www.clubtiger.com>   <http://www.infoplease.com>
<http://www.go.ESPN.com>   <http://www.NYTimes.com>
<http://www.golf.com>   <http://www.tigerwoods.com>
<http://www.golfweb.com>   <http://www.texnews.com/tiger>

FOR FURTHER READING

Anderson, Dave. *The Story of Golf.* New York: William Morrow, 1998.

Christopher, Matt. *On the Course with . . . Tiger Woods.* New York: Little, Brown & Company, 1998.

Clary, Jack. *Tiger Woods.* Wilton, CT: Belden Hill Press, 1997.

Edwards, Nicholas. *Tiger Woods: An American Master.* New York: Scholastic Books, 1997.

Garrity, John. *Tiger Woods: The Making of a Champion.* New York: Simon & Schuster, 1996.

Gutman, Bill. *Tiger Woods.* New York: Pocket Books, 1997.

Savage, Jeff. *Tiger Woods, King of the Course.* Minneapolis, MN: Lerner Publications Company, 1998.

Strege, John. *Tiger.* New York: Broadway Books, 1997.

Woods, Earl, with Shari Lesser Wenk and the Tiger Woods Foundation. *Start Something.* New York: Simon & Schuster, 2000.

WEBSITES

<http://www.clubtiger.com> (Official fan site produced by CBS Sportsline. Registration required. Users must be over thirteen.)

<http://www.golf.com/golfindex.fhtml?/bios.woods_tiger> (Golf.com statistics related to Tiger's performance)

<http://www.golfweb.com/players/intro/8793.html> (PGA Tour page with Tiger's official biography and PGA statistics)

<http://www.infoplease.com/spot/tigertime1.html> (Timeline of Tiger's career)

<http://www.tigerwoods.com> (Official site produced by CBS Sportsline)

GLOSSARY

address: the point at which the golfer takes his or her stance and prepares to swing the club

backswing: the motion of a golfer's hands, arms, and body as he or she pulls the club back before hitting the ball. The backswing creates the power for the shot.

birdie: a score that is one shot lower than par on a hole

bogey: a score that is one shot higher than par on a hole

bunker: a small depression on a fairway or next to a green, usually filled with sand. If filled with sand, it is also called a sand trap.

caddie: the person who carries a golfer's bag and keeps track of distances and conditions. When asked, the caddie offers the golfer advice and encouragement.

chip shot: a short, easy shot. It can be to the green from the fairway or from the woods to an area back in play.

chunking: when a golfer erroneously hits the ground with the clubhead before it strikes the ball. This unpleasant maneuver is also called "stubbing," "scuffing," "dunching," and "sclaffing."

cup: the actual hole on the green into which the ball is hit

divot: a piece of turf dug up by a golf swing. Players are expected to replace divots immediately.

double bogey: a score that is two shots higher than par on a hole

drive: the first shot hit by a golfer on each hole

driving range: an area where golfers practice their swings and drives. These practice areas usually have distance markers, allowing the golfers to see how far they have hit their ball.

eagle: a score that is two shots lower than par on a hole

fried egg: a ball in a sand trap that kicked a lot of sand away when it landed so that the ball sits in the center of a small hole and looks like a fried egg

handicap: the average number of strokes over par a golfer normally plays. The lower the handicap, the better the golfer. The handicap is subtracted from the final score to see who wins. This system is used so that players of different abilities can compete against each other. Professional competitions do not use handicaps.

hazards: anything in the area of play that can make playing more difficult for a golfer. Bunkers are common hazards, but natural features, such as rocks or trees, can also be hazards.

head: the end of the golf club that hits the ball. The face is the surface that actually strikes the golf ball. The shape and size of the head varies with the type of club.

hook shot: a drive that curves from right to left while in the air. This curving action often puts the ball into a difficult area to play.

iron: a metal club with a grooved, angled head. The angle allows a golfer to give a shot loft.

iron game: shots made with irons. This term usually refers to the middle of each hole, after a drive from the tee.

lie of the ball: where the ball stops. A good lie means that a ball is placed well for the next shot to the green or the cup.

par: the number of shots a golfer is expected to use to complete a hole

pitch shot: a short, high-angle shot made with an iron and often used to get on the green or avoid a hazard

putt: a stroke used on the green, designed to roll the ball into the cup. Putts can be deceptively difficult.

reading the green: trying to determine how a ball will travel on the green. The slope of the green and other factors, such as the wind, make this critical step difficult on most putts.

tee: a small wooden or plastic T-shaped peg, used to elevate the golf ball to make it easier to hit. The tee is used only at the start of each hole.

teeing off: taking the first shot on each hole. The golfer puts the ball on a tee before hitting it. The golfer may place the tee and the ball anywhere on the tee box, or marked area at the start of the hole. Two markers usually designate the tee box. There are often different tee boxes for men, women, and young golfers.

waggle: the movements a golfer makes before starting his or her swing to relieve tension or nervousness

whiff: swinging and missing the ball

wood: a club with a large head and a flat face, which allows a golfer to drive the ball very far. The heads of these clubs were originally made of wood. In modern times, metals are generally used.

yips: a case of nervousness so severe that it causes the player to lose control of his or her hands

INDEX

OTHER TITLES FROM LERNER AND A&E®:

Arthur Ashe
The Beatles
Benjamin Franklin
Bill Gates
Carl Sagan
Chief Crazy Horse
Christopher Reeve
Daring Pirate Women
Edgar Allan Poe
Eleanor Roosevelt
George W. Bush
George Lucas
Gloria Estefan
Jack London
Jacques Cousteau
Jane Austen
Jesse Owens
Jesse Ventura
Jimi Hendrix
John Glenn
Latin Sensations
Legends of Dracula

Legends of Santa Claus
Louisa May Alcott
Madeleine Albright
Malcolm X
Mark Twain
Maya Angelou
Mohandas Gandhi
Mother Teresa
Nelson Mandela
Oprah Winfrey
Princess Diana
Queen Cleopatra
Queen Elizabeth I
Queen Latifah
Rosie O'Donnell
Saint Joan of Arc
Thurgood Marshall
William Shakespeare
Wilma Rudolph
Women in Space
Women of the Wild West

ABOUT THE AUTHOR

Jeremy Roberts is the pen name of Jim DeFelice. He often uses this name when he writes for young readers, which he tries to do as often as he can. In addition to this A&E® BIOGRAPHY, Roberts has written two other books in this series, *Saint Joan of Arc* and *The Beatles*. His recent nonfiction books include works on skydiving and rock climbing. His adult books include a historical trilogy and techno-thrillers. He lives with his wife and son in a haunted farmhouse in New York.

PHOTO ACKNOWLEDGMENTS

Photographs used with the permission of: © ALLSPORT USA/Donald Miralle, p. 2; © David Strick/CORBIS OUTLINE, pp. 6, 18, 26; © ALLSPORT USA/Ken Levine, p. 8; AP/Wide World Photos, pp. 9, 56, 65; © Bettmann/CORBIS, p. 10; © Van der Heyden Collection/Independent Picture Service, pp. 13, 29; © ALLSPORT USA/Craig Jones, pp. 14, 71; © Todd Strand/Independent Picture Service, p. 16; © Duomo/CORBIS, pp. 23, 40, 78; *San Diego Union-Tribune*/Dave Siccardi, p. 28; © ALLSPORT USA/Rusty Jarrett, p. 32; © ALLSPORT USA/Jamie Squire, pp. 38, 53; © Morton Beebe, S.F./CORBIS, p. 43; © ALLSPORT USA/Joe Patronite, p. 45; © ALLSPORT USA/J.D. Cuban, p. 48; © ALLSPORT USA/Stephen Munday, p. 62; © ALLSPORT USA/Doug Pensinger, p. 68; © ALLSPORT USA/Harry How, pp. 72, 92; © ALLSPORT USA/Vincent Laforet, p. 74; © AFP/CORBIS, pp. 82, 86; © Reuters NewMedia, Inc./CORBIS, pp. 84, 89, 96; © ALLSPORT USA/ David Cannon, p. 94.

Hard cover: front, © ALLSPORT USA/Andrew Redington; back, © Reuters NewMedia, Inc./CORBIS;
Soft cover: front, © Reuters NewMedia, Inc./CORBIS; back, © ALLSPORT USA/Craig Jones